MIRTH
FOR THE
MILLENNIUM

Cal and Rose Samra

WATERBROOK
PRESS

MIRTH FOR THE MILLENNIUM
PUBLISHED BY WATERBROOK PRESS
5446 North Academy Boulevard, Suite 200
Colorado Springs, Colorado 80918
A division of Random House, Inc.

For information about the Fellowship of Merry Christians and *The Joyful Noiseletter,*
please call toll-free 1-800-877-2757 from 8 A.M. to 5 P.M. E.S.T. M-F or write:
FMC, PO Box 895, Portage, MI 49081-0895. E-mail: JoyfulNZ@aol.com
Visit FMC's website: www.JoyfulNoiseletter.com

Library of Congress Cataloging-in-Publication Data
Mirth for the millennium / [compiled by] Cal and Rosa Samra.
          p.   cm.
     ISBN 1-57856-283-X
     1. Millennium Humor.   2. Millennialism Humor.   3. End of the world
Humor.   I. Samra, Cal.   II. Samra, Rose.
PN6231.M52M57   1999
230′.002′7—dc21   99-33686
                                                                  CIP

Printed in the United States of America
1999—First Edition

10 9 8 7 6 5 4 3 2 1

*"Mirth is like a flash of lightning
that breaks through a gloom of clouds
and glitters for the moment.
Cheerfulness keeps up a daylight in the mind,
filling it with steady and perpetual serenity."*

—SAMUEL JOHNSON

PREFACE

In the year 2000, the Fellowship of Merry Christians, publishers of the monthly *The Joyful Noiseletter*, will celebrate our fifteenth anniversary.

We invite people to join us in greeting the new millennium with joy and laughter.

John 16:33 notes that Jesus called us to "be of good cheer." We think that we should make an effort to "be of good cheer" from century to century, notwithstanding the circumstances.

This little book is our contribution to the millennium celebration.

God bless and smile on you in the new millennium!

—CAL AND ROSE SAMRA
EDITORS, *THE JOYFUL NOISELETTER*

An angel of the Lord telephoned the editors of major news media and informed them that the world will end tomorrow. Here are the front-page headlines that subsequently appeared:

- *The New York Times*: "The World Will End Tomorrow, Reliable Source Says." (A box read: "Analysis on page 11.")
- *The Washington Post*: "World Ends Tomorrow; Congress Approves Term-Limits, School Prayer."
- *The Washington Times*: "End of World Linked to Monica, Democrats."
- *New Republic*: "End of World Linked to Republican Contract with America."
- *Wall Street Journal*: "World Ends Tomorrow; Dow Tops All-Time High."
- *USA Today*: "We're Gone!"

- *Sports Illustrated:* "Game's Over."
- *Ladies' Home Journal:* "Lose 10 Pounds by Judgment Day with Our New Armageddon Diet!"
- *Fortune* Magazine: "Ten Ways You Can Profit from the Apocalypse."
- CNN: "World Ends: Women and Children Most Affected."
- Penney's Catalog: "Our Final Sale."
- America Online: "System Temporarily Down. Try Calling Back in 15 Minutes."

⑥

A paramedic was asked on a local TV talk-show program: "What was your most unusual and challenging 911 call?"

"Recently, we got a call from that big white church at 11th and Walnut," the paramedic said. "A frantic usher was very concerned that during the sermon an elderly man passed out in a pew and appeared to be dead. The usher could find no pulse and there was no noticeable breathing."

"What was so unusual and demanding about this particular call?" the interviewer asked.

"Well," the paramedic said, "we carried out four guys before we found the one who was dead."

—VIA KARL M. HARSNEY, BATH, PENNSYLVANIA

On the wall of the men's room at a Kansas truck stop were scribbled the words: "If God be for us, who can be against us?"

Scrawled beneath, someone had added: "The highway patrol!"

—MSGR. ARTHUR TONNE, *JOKES PRIESTS CAN TELL*

Question: What's the difference between Noah's ark and the *Titanic*?
Answer: An amateur built Noah's ark. The *Titanic* was built by professionals.

—VIA REV. KARL R. KRAFT, MANTUA, NEW JERSEY

Sign on the outside wall of a Maryland convent:
   "Trespassers Will Be Prosecuted
   to the Fullest Extent of the Law."
      —*The Sisters of Mercy*

A confirmation student was asked to list the Ten Commandments in any order: He wrote: "3, 6, 1, 8, 4, 5, 9, 2, 10, 7."

Question: How many prophets does it take to screw in a light bulb?
Answer: Two. One to screw in the light bulb and one to curse him for living in darkness.

—BRIAN IRVING, THE RALEIGH, NORTH CAROLINA, LIMEX GROUP

"If some of these folks would spend their time following His example instead of trying to figure out His mode of arrival and departure, they would come nearer getting confidence in their church."

—WILL ROGERS

Pastor Mike McClung of Lionheart Fellowship in Maryville, Tennessee, passed along the following "proof that Barney is the Antichrist" in hopes that he might wring a laugh out of prophecy students:

1. Start with the given:
   CUTE PURPLE DINOSAUR
2. Change all the U's to V's (which is proper Latin anyway):
   CVTE PVRPLE DINOSAVR
3. Extract all the Roman Numerals:
   CVVLDIV
4. Convert these to Arabic values:
   100-5-5-50-500-1-5
5. Add them up:
   666

A certain church found itself burdened with a very tedious and self-centered pastor for a couple of years. Then came the day when he was called to another church. He announced his resignation by saying, "Brethren, the same Lord who sent me to you is now calling me away."

After a moment's silence, suddenly the congregation rose as one and began to sing, "What a Friend We Have in Jesus."

—TAL BONHAM

"If man evolved from monkeys and apes, why do we still have monkeys and apes?"

—VIA PATTY WOOTEN, RN, SANTA CRUZ, CALIFORNIA

A Buddhist Zen master went up to a hot dog vendor at a baseball game and said: "Make me one with everything."

When the Zen master paid with a twenty-dollar bill, the hot dog vendor put the bill in the cash drawer.

"Where's my change?" the Zen master asked.

"Change must come from within," the hot dog vendor replied.

⌬

After a worship service, a preacher announced: "The class on prophecy has been canceled due to unforeseen circumstances."

—GEORGE GOLDTRAP, ORMOND-BY-THE-SEA, FLORIDA

"In the Bible, the words 'fear not' can be found 365 times: once for every day of the year."

—VIA CATHERINE HALL, PITTSBURGH, PENNSYLVANIA

"People *love* the Bigfoot of myth. Do you want to destroy it by revealing that I'm just a hairy hermit trying to find God?"

© Ed Sullivan

A British recluse named Ernest Digweed died in the early 1980s and left the equivalent of fifty-seven thousand dollars in his will for Jesus Christ if He should return to earth before the end of the twentieth century. Digweed's heirs asked the courts to invalidate the will and divide the money among them. The judges agreed but they took out insurance with Lloyds of London for the amount just in case Christ does return within Digweed's stipulated time.

—WILLIAM J. FREBURGER

"I'm convinced there is only one place where there is no laughter—and that's hell. I have made arrangements to miss hell. Praise God! I won't ever have to be anywhere that there ain't no laughter."

—COMEDIAN JERRY CLOWER, *LIFE EVERLAUGHTER*

"If you're not allowed to laugh in heaven, I don't want to go there."

—MARTIN LUTHER

A PRAYER FOR GOOD CHEER

"Father, save me from the depression that comes from accepting every gloomy prediction and every bad news story as though they were the whole truth. May your grace help me not to be anxious about tomorrow, but to live with the trust that enables me to cope with today."

—REGINALD HOLLIS, *THE ANGLICAN DIGEST*

One day in the cathedral a very excited young priest approached a cardinal. "Your Eminence," the priest cried, "a woman claims to have seen a vision of the Savior in the chapel. What should we do?"

"Look busy," the cardinal said. "Look busy."

—SOPHIA BAR

Seen on a bumper sticker in Indianapolis:
"Jesus Is Coming! Look Busy!

"Be joyful in the Lord, and merry."

—ST. FRANCIS OF ASSISI

Aaron Wymer, a minister for a Disciples of Christ church, told this story to a group of students at Florida Tech in Melbourne, Florida:

A man had been shipwrecked on a remote island in the Pacific and was alone for twenty years. When a ship finally arrived, his rescuers were impressed with the three buildings he had built and asked him about them.

"Well," the man replied, "this is my house, and that building over there is my church. It's a wonderful church; and I hate to leave it."

"And what is the third building yonder?" a rescuer asked.

"Oh, that is the church I used to go to," the man replied.

—VIA PALMER STILES, MELBOURNE, FLORIDA

One of our church deacons at the Baptist church in Auburn, Alabama, was a barber who felt guilty because he had never witnessed for the Lord. One day a man came into his barbershop and asked for a shave.

The barber put him in a chair and lathered his face. He thought this would be the perfect time to witness to the customer. Nervously, he asked,

"SSSir, are you rrready to mmmeet the LLLord?"

The man opened his eyes wide and saw the barber holding the razor with a shaking hand. He jumped out of his chair and took off running down the street with the haircloth flapping in the wind.

—LEE SWOPE, AUBURN, ALABAMA

An atheist was sailing in Scotland when the Loch Ness monster suddenly attacked his boat. The monster flipped the sailboat in the air and opened its mouth to swallow him.

"Oh God, help me!" the man cried out. The monster froze and backed off. The man heard laughter and a deep voice from the sky declare, "I thought you didn't believe in Me!"

"Give me a break, God," the man replied. "Until a minute ago, I didn't believe in the Loch Ness Monster either."

—VIA LOIS H. WARD, PROSPECT, OHIO

"Thank you for that message on the Apocalypse, pastor. Now, let's all stand and sing, 'We'll Understand It Better Bye And Bye.'"

© Dennis Daniel

A member of his congregation told Rev. Warren J. Keating, pastor of First Presbyterian Church, Derby, Kansas, that this was the best prayer he ever heard:

"Dear God, please help me be the person my dog thinks I am."

⑥

Two sailors were adrift on a raft in the ocean. They had just about given up hope of rescue. One began to pray: "O Lord, I've led a worthless life and neglected my children and been unkind to my wife, but if you'll save me, I promise I…"

"Hold it!" the other shouted. "I think I see land!"

—MARGARET HARRIS, GRAND RAPIDS, MICHIGAN

The late Archbishop John L. May of St. Louis told this story:

Down in Southern Missouri, we have the Ozarks and the people down there don't know much about Catholics.

A priest's car stalled on a back road, and he went to a small house to find help. The nice couple there said they had never met anyone with a collar on backwards.

The priest said, "Then how come you have a picture of the pope on the wall?"

"Where?" they asked. The priest pointed to a picture on the wall. It was a picture of Pope Pius XII, a former pope who wore glasses.

"Who's that?" they asked.

"The pope," the priest said.

"Oh, my gosh!" the couple exclaimed. "We were told that was Harry Truman in his 33rd-degree Masonic outfit."

Coming through the church just before the service was scheduled to begin, a bishop noted with some displeasure that there was a very sparse congregation.

"There are not many people in church today," the bishop said to the rector. "Did you tell them I was coming?"

"No, bishop," the rector replied. "Someone else must have."

—REV. J. STEPHEN HINES, *EASY ON THE ALLELUIAS, HARRY*

Overheard in the sacristy:

"The congregation's a bit thin this morning," said the vicar. "Did you tell them I was preaching?"

"No, Vicar, I didn't," replied the churchwarden, "but you know how things get out."

—*THE ANGLICAN DIGEST*

"Laughter is the joyous universal evergreen of life."
—ABRAHAM LINCOLN

"If no one ever took risks, Michelangelo would have painted the Sistine floor."

—NEIL SIMON

"Some visitors to Calcutta asked me to tell them something that would be useful for them to lead their lives in a more profitable way. I answered, 'Smile at each other. Smile at your wives, at your husbands, at your children, at all. Let mutual love for others grow each day in all of you.'"

—MOTHER TERESA, *HEART OF JOY*

"I love California! Tremors give me a lot of great sermon ideas about the instability of the world."

A pastor for a small church was so poorly paid that he began to look for a part-time job to help support his family. He saw an ad in the newspaper for a worker at the local zoo.

He applied and was told by the zoo manager, "The black bear has always been one of our prime attractions, but he died a week ago. We want someone to come in three or four days every week, dress as a black bear, and entertain the kids."

The preacher got the job, and he made a good bear. He'd growl and run around the bear cage, and everyone thought he was a real bear.

One day he decided to climb the tree like a bear. The kids loved it.

Unfortunately, the fake tree was not properly secured. It tilted over, and the bear fell into the lion's den.

The lion pounced on the bear. The clawing, biting lion was too much for the bear. The preacher decided that the only way he could survive was to hug the lion as tightly as he could. He squeezed so hard that the lion could hardly breathe.

Finally, the lion shouted: "Ease up, brother! You're not the only underpaid preacher in town!"

—VIA GEORGE GOLDTRAP, ORMOND-BY-THE-SEA, FLORIDA

"Our Advent wreath at St. Timothy Cumberland Presbyterian Church in Bedford, Texas, has the traditional five candles, four of which have mechanical springs. The altar committee trims the candles to fit, retracts the spring mechanisms, and inserts the candles. As they burn, the spring pressure automatically pushes the candles up.

"During the Advent season last year, the altar committee was unavailable to prepare the candles, and so the pastor took it upon himself to replace the old candles. Unable to find the appropriate straight candles, he chose four new tapered ones and inserted them into the spring mechanisms with the fat ends up.

"A test lighting worked beautifully, and all went well for the first three Sundays in Advent. But on the fourth Sunday in Advent, midway through the pastor's sermon, the congregation was startled to hear a loud 'snap.' They watched one candle skyrocket all the way to the rafters, then fall to the floor.

"Unruffled, the pastor continued his sermon. There was another snap, and a second candle soared into the heavens, then landed—still burning. There was a mad dash of the elders to put out the burning candle and snuff out the other candles before they, too, were launched.

"The fourth Sunday in Advent turned out to look like the Fourth of July.

But the pastor, amid the congregation's laughter, continued to preach in 'decent and good order.'"

—Pastor Barney Hudson
St. Timothy Cumberland Presbyterian Church,
Bedford, Texas

From London, Bob White sent this "Poem in Praise of a Successful Preacher" from the publication of St. Andrew's and St. Michael's Parishes (Church of England):

> We gave him twenty minutes,
>   and he finished up in ten.
> Oh, there's a prince of speakers
>   and a servant unto men!
> His diction wasn't very much;
>   he hemmed and hawed a bit.
> Still he spoke a lot of sense
>   and after that he quit.
> At first we sat quite paralyzed,
>   then cheered and cheered again.
> We gave him twenty minutes,
>   and he finished up in ten.

You know you are in the wrong church when...
- The church bulletin lists the senior pastor, the associate pastor, and the psycho-pastor.
- The choir wears black leather robes with studded collars.
- During the offering, you observe that all of the ushers are armed.

—VIA REV. KARL R. KRAFT, MANTUA, NEW JERSEY

"It is only believers in the fall of Man who can really appreciate how funny men are. Love laughter, which sounds loudly as heaven's gates swing open, and dies away as they shut."

—MALCOLM MUGGERIDGE

"Welcome to the real Moral Majority, Bixley."

Rev. Robert A. Pollauf, SJ, of Sts. Peter and Paul Church, Detroit, passes on this account of how Daniel survived in the lions' den:

King Nebuchadnezzar of Babylon was astonished that the hungry lions had not eaten Daniel. He summoned Daniel and promised him that if he would reveal his secret, the king would give him his freedom.

"It was easy, Your Excellency," Daniel said. "I went around and whispered in each lion's ear—'After dinner, there will be speeches.'"

When a Bible salesman was asked how he consistently sold more Bibles than anyone else, he replied: "I jjjust aaasked eeeach pppprospect if he wwwanted to bbbuy a Bbbible or hhhave me rrread it to hhhim."

—JIM REED

An old, retired professor of church history at Yale was on his deathbed. Waiting relatives anxiously gathered around him.

After a time of silence one man quietly said: "I think he's gone."

Another relative, standing at the end of the bed, felt the old man's feet and said, "No, his feet are still warm. No one ever dies with warm feet."

The eyes of the old professor blinked open. He raised his head up from the bed and looked around at his family. "Joan of Arc did!" he whispered. He gave a little chuckle and died.

—JERIS BRAGAN, *NEW COVENANT*

Adam was very lonely in the Garden of Eden and told God he had to have someone besides God to talk to. God replied that He would give Adam a companion—a woman.

God said the woman would cook for Adam, wash his clothes, clean his home, bear his children, and take care of them.

The woman, God said, would always agree with every decision Adam made and never argue with him. She would be full of love for him, and she would heal his wounds. She would never have a headache, and she would always be in good humor.

"What will a woman like this cost me?" Adam asked.

"An arm and a leg," God replied.

"What can I get for just a rib?" Adam asked.

—VIA BUD FRIMOTH, PORTLAND, OREGON

"Today may the sun shine on your world;
may the rain fall on your garden;
may the clouds pass over your troubles;
may the stars twinkle on your life;
may the moon brighten your journey;
and may tonight bring you a better tomorrow."
   —*Old Irish Blessing*

—VIA REV. JOHN H. FAHEY, WASHINGTON,
WEST VIRGINIA

An elderly priest, who had spent fifty years preaching in parish missions, dreamed one night that he died and knocked on the pearly gates.

"Who is there?" St. Peter asked.

"I am Fr. Clyde, preacher of missions for over fifty years."

"Ah, yes, Fr. Clyde," St. Peter said. "I'm sorry, but you can't come in yet. First you will have to spend three months in purgatory."

"Three months in purgatory!" the priest exclaimed. "I spent my life preaching missions all over Australia!"

"Please be calm, father," St. Peter said. "You won't have to work. We have a comfortable chair for you in a comfortable room. You won't have to do anything except listen to your own sermons day and night. We taped all the sermons you preached at those missions…"

The priest woke up in a sweat.

—VIA FR. JIM CARROLL, OMI
    BLESSED EUGENE DE MAZENOD PARISH, BURPENGARY,
    AUSTRALIA

"As a Catholic, I've tried to explain purgatory to non-Catholics. Purgatory is a place between heaven and hell. It's like you're stuck between floors on an elevator, and this elevator is jammed full of people who have just been to Taco Bell for lunch. You're going to get to that top floor eventually, but it's not going to be a pleasant ride. They understand that."

—TOMMY DINARDO, CATHOLIC COMEDIAN,
VIRGINIA BEACH, VIRGINIA

> *"From somber, serious, sullen saints, save us,*
> *O Lord. Lord, hear our prayer."*
>
> —ST. TERESA OF AVILA (A.D. 1582)

"The motion we participate in Unity Sunday passes 6–5."

"A committee is a gathering of important people who singly can do nothing, but together can decide that nothing can be done."

—COMEDIAN FRED ALLEN

"It's always a consolation to me to realize that although God created man and woman, there is no recorded testimony that He created committees. For this alone we worship Him."

—JOHN V. CHERVOKAS

Sign seen outside the Needier Church of Christ in Haleyville, Alabama:

"God so loved the world
that He did not send a committee."

When God was creating the animals, a group of angels remarked that it looked like fun, so God let them form a committee and create one animal. The committee created the platypus—an animal with the bill of a duck, the fur of an otter, the tail of a beaver, and the feet of a frog.

"Enough!" said God, and ever since there have been no committees in heaven.

—MSGR. JOSEPH P. DOOLEY, MARTINS CREEK,
PENNSYLVANIA

"In heaven, there are no meetings. In purgatory, there are long meetings three times a week. Hell is just one unending meeting."

—VIA FR. GEORGE BIRGE
ST. ROSE PARISH, NEWTON, CONNECTICUT

The Eleventh Commandment: "Thou shalt not committee."

—TAL BONHAM

"Outside of traffic, there is nothing that has held this country back as much as committees."

—WILL ROGERS

"Search your parks in all your cities; you'll find no statues of committees."

—DAVID OGILVY

A local bishop was the speaker at a banquet for single women and widows. More than 150 women attended. The centerpieces on the tables were given to the women who had a number on the back of their chairs.

The bishop expressed his regrets that not everyone got to take something home, so he told each of the women to pick a number between 1 and 150 because there are 150 chapters in Psalms. Then everyone would have something to take home.

One older woman, not understanding that they were to keep the numbers to themselves, called out, "Fifty-six."

The bishop said he would read the psalm to the group. The first verse:

"Be merciful to me, O God, for men hotly pursue me; all day long they press their attack!"

—VIA IDA MAE GEHMAN, PALMYRA, PENNSYLVANIA

An Episcopal diocesan bishop went to an unfamiliar church to celebrate the Eucharist. Uncertain whether the microphone on the altar was switched on, he tapped it gently with no result. So leaning very close to it, he said in a loud whisper that echoed around the church: "There must be something wrong with this microphone."

The well-trained and responsive congregation, very familiar with the latest in liturgical language, replied at once, "And also with you."

—BULLETIN OF THE PARISH OF COLEY, HALIFAX

"Aim at the cheerfulness of faith."

—JOHN WESLEY

Helping his wife wash the dishes, a minister protested, "This isn't a man's job."

"Oh yes, it is," his wife retorted, quoting 2 Kings 21:13—"I will wipe Jerusalem as a man wipeth a dish, wiping it, and turning it upside down."

—TAL BONHAM

"Anybody who has ever used the expression, 'It was no Sunday school picnic' has obviously never been to a Sunday school picnic."

—VIA REV. RONALD H. WEINELT
ST. JOHN'S LUTHERAN CHURCH, RINCON, GEORGIA

TOP TEN SIGNS YOU'RE IN A DRY-BONES CHURCH

10. The choir director and the organist quit and no one notices for three months.

9. The baptismal is now being used for chips and dip in the social hall.

8. The pew Bibles donated a year ago still have the cellophane on them.

7. The pastor takes a month-long sabbatical and is told upon his return that his sermons over the last month have been better than ever.

6. The custodian passes away while cleaning the sanctuary and no one realizes it for three weeks.

5. The pastor has been using the same Scripture passage as his/her text for two months.

4. The pulpit was moved six inches to the left and twenty-five people volunteer to serve on the task force to investigate.

3. The altar rail has not been cleaned since the custodian passed away.

2. The nursery is being used for long-term storage.

1. Jesus Christ visited and was told He was sitting in someone's seat.

—REV. JEFF HANNA
FIRST UNITED METHODIST CHURCH, GALION, OHIO

Top Ten Ways to Tell If a Church Is Spirit-filled

10. You have to assign numbers to people who want to share their testimony in worship.

9. As the pastor closes the sermon, the chant of "We want more! We want more!" erupts.

8. The ushers have to empty the collection plates halfway through the offering because they are too full.

7. The choir begins to sing and can't stop.

6. Members begin buying new Bibles because they wore the others out.

5. There is an influx of people asking, "Is there something I can do?"

4. New classes and small groups have to be formed because so many people want to teach.

3. People offer their seats to newcomers.

2. New altar rails have to be installed to handle the crowds.

1. The congregation douses the pastor with a cooler of water at the end of the service.

—REV. JEFF HANNA

Ad in the *Ellsworth* (Wisconsin) *American:* "Village Dry Cleaners has relocated to 14 High Street, right next door to St. Joseph's Church. After March 1, cleanliness *is* next to godliness."

—ROBERT WAGNER, MILWAUKEE, WISCONSIN

"Very few people realize this, but the corner-stone of this church is actually a fruitcake given to me by Ethel Mabeline during the Christmas of '72."

© Jonny Hawkins

Seen on an outdoor church sign:

"The Lord is seeking righteous fruit, not religious nuts."

—VIA REV. LARRY CRAWFORD
WESTLAKE CHRISTIAN FELLOWSHIP,
ST. CHARLES, MARYLAND

Woman to pastor: "You don't know how much your sermons have meant to my husband since he lost his mind."

—TAL BONHAM

You can always identify the pastor of any parish. He's the one who goes around and turns out the lights. Two young priests were discussing how penurious their senior pastor was. Said one: "When he dies, if he sees a light at the end of the tunnel, he'll put it out."

—MSGR. CHARLES DOLLEN, *THE PRIEST*

THE PASTOR AND THE GENIE

A young pastor was walking in his backyard when his toe struck what appeared to be an old lamp buried in the ground. When he picked it up, a genie dressed in rags suddenly popped out.

The genie was annoyed that he had been awakened. "Okay," he said, "tell me your one wish and make it quick. I want to get back into the lamp."

"I've always dreamed of this happening," the pastor said excitedly. "Stay right here. I'll be back in a minute." Soon he returned with a map of the Middle East, unfolded it, and showed it to the genie.

"My one wish is that peace and harmony will come to this whole area, from the Balkans and Turkey to Egypt, from Israel to Iraq and Iran," the pastor said.

"Are you crazy?" the genie exclaimed. "Give me a break. I'm an old genie, and the Middle East has been in strife and at war for thousands of years. I just can't do it!"

The pastor thought for a while and then said, "Okay, I'll make another request. I wish that my church would be a place where everyone could live in peace, where everyone would love and respect one another, and there would no longer be any bickering, petty feuding, and quarreling."

The genie pondered the request and then said, "Do you mind if I take another look at that map?"

—Rev. Robert M. Ross
St. Peter's Episcopal Church,
Ostervillle, Maryland

Moses had a press agent named Sam. When he and his people got to the Red Sea with the Pharaoh's armies in hot pursuit, he called for Sam and asked: "Where are the boats?"

"Oh, I'm sorry, Moses," Sam said. "I was so busy with the press releases, newspapers, and bookings, I forgot to order the boats."

"You idiot!" Moses exclaimed. "What do you want me to do—raise my staff and ask God to part the Red Sea?"

"Hey, Boss," Sam said, "If you can do that, I could get you two pages in the Old Testament."

—STEVE FELDMAN, JEFFERSON CITY, MISSOURI

Comedian Steve Allen, a consulting editor to The Joyful Noiseletter, *sent the following story:*

During an ecumenical gathering, someone rushed in shouting, "The building is on fire!"

- The Methodists at once gathered in a corner and prayed.
- The Baptists cried, "Everybody into the water."
- The Lutherans posted a notice on the door declaring that fire was evil because it was the natural abode of the devil.
- The Congregationalists shouted, "Every man for himself!"
- The Seventh-Day Adventists proclaimed, "It's the vengeance of an angry God!"
- The Christian Scientists agreed among themselves that there really was not a fire.

- The Presbyterians appointed a chairperson, who was to appoint a committee to look into the matter and make a written report to the session.
- The Episcopalians formed a procession and marched out in good order.
- The Unitarian-Universalists concluded that the fire had as much right to be there as anyone else.
- The Catholics passed a collection plate to cover the damages.

Classified ad in Rev. David R. Francoeur's whimsical Ecclesiastical Times, *published irregularly in Stuart, Florida:*

Middle East Diocese looking for candidates for Bishop. Must be athletic, agile, and have great endurance. Former track stars preferred. Salary and benefits negotiable. Package includes bunker and armored personnel carrier for Sunday visitations. Must be willing to relocate. Interested parties reply to: TET, Box 12-V.

"I believe we're on earth to delight each other, make each other laugh, and to infuse one another with His joy. Why not? What've we got better to do?"

—COMEDIAN BURT ROSENBERG, SILVER SPRING, MARYLAND

"Humor is a divine quality, and God has the greatest sense of humor of all. He must have; otherwise He wouldn't have made so many politicians."

—MARTIN LUTHER KING

I love a finished speaker,
I really, really do.
I don't mean one who's polished.
I just mean one who's through.

—REV. BERNARD BRUNSTING

"Whence comes this idea that if what we are doing is fun, it can't be God's will? The God who made giraffes, a baby's fingernails, a puppy's tail, a crooknecked squash, the bobwhite's call, and a young girl's giggle has a sense of humor. Make no mistake about that."

—CATHERINE MARSHALL

I think that I shall never see
A church that's all it ought to be;
A church whose members never stray
Beyond the straight and narrow way;
A church whose members always sing
And flock to church when bells ring.
Such perfect churches there may be,
But none of them are known to me.
But still we'll work and pray and plan
To make our own the best we can.

—MSGR. JOSEPH P. DOOLEY
ST. ROCCO'S CHURCH, MARTINS CREEK, PENNSYLVANIA

Ecumenism: Getting to know the opposite sects.

—RON BIRK, SAN MARCOS, TEXAS

"Don't call anyone sinners until after the collection."

© Harley L. Schwadron

Reading the Sunday Scripture on the coming of the Wise Men from Matthew 2:11, a deacon said, "And they presented him with gifts of gold, frankincense, and mirth."

A pastor observed: "We certainly believe in the Resurrection at our church. If you doubt it, just visit our offices sometime and watch our staff come back to life at quitting time."

"No one would have been invited to dinner as often as Jesus was unless He was interesting and had a sense of humor."

—CHARLES M. SCHULTZ

40 years of ministry prepared Pastor Lou for
his retirement years.

© Steve Phelps

WHY GOD NEVER RECEIVED TENURE AT A UNIVERSITY

Joyful Noiseletter *consulting editors Steve Feldman of Jefferson City, Missouri, and George and Peggy Goldtrap of Ormond-by-the-Sea, Florida, put their heads together and came up with "Seventeen Reasons Why God Never Received Tenure at a University."*

1. He published only one book.
2. Some scholars seriously doubt that He wrote it Himself.
3. It was first published in Hebrew, then in Greek, and then endlessly revised and rewritten by translators.
4. It carried no references and was never published in an authorized journal.
5. He was vague about His background and credentials and kept repeating, "I am that I am."

6. He was repeatedly accused of being a male chauvinist.

7. He would not submit to psychological examinations or psychotherapy conducted by one of His peers.

8. He did not keep regular office hours and sometimes insisted on holding His classes on mountaintops.

9. He wanted ten percent of the university's income as His salary.

10. He never got permission from the National Institutes of Health to experiment with human subjects.

11. He put His first student to sleep.

12. He expelled His first two students.

13. He insisted on ten rules for maintaining campus discipline.

14. He gave final exams on the honor system.

15. He refused to grade on a curve.
16. He sent His Son to teach the class.
17. Scientists cannot replicate His results.

On Thanksgiving Day, FMC member Bill Reynolds of Palatka, Florida, saw this outdoor church sign as he drove by a church:

> *"11-26-97 Services Canceled.*
> *In Everything Give Thanks."*

"The road to hell is paved with good conventions."

— GEORGE GOLDTRAP

Rev. Vincent Heier, of the Catholic Archdiocese of St. Louis, welcomed a group of Missouri-Kansas Lutherans meeting in St. Louis Cathedral with these words:

"We are pleased to provide the cathedral. Please don't nail anything to the doors."

When Pope Pius XII was still a monsignor, he told this story:

A certain abbess, the head of a female monastery, insisted that the priest-chaplain of the monastery kiss her hand when meeting her. He refused. The matter was referred to Rome, which gave this decision, translated from Latin: "The chaplain is not bound to kiss the abbess, but let him make merely a slight inclination of the head as to an old relic."

—MSGR. ARTHUR TONNE, *JOKES PRIESTS CAN TELL*

Laugh and be merry:
Remember, in olden time,
God made Heaven and Earth for joy,
He took in a rhyme, made them,
And filled them full
with the strong red wine of his mirth.
The splendid joy of the stars:
The joy of the earth.

—JOHN MASEFIELD

A woman went to the post office to buy stamps for her Christmas cards. "What denomination?" asked the clerk.

"Oh, good heavens! Have we come to this?" said the woman. "Well, give me fifty Catholic and fifty Baptist ones."

—VIA PASTOR JIM PATRICK, INDIANOLA, IOWA

"Bring some zest into your life in the New Millennium! Make a friend; fall in love; paint a picture, write a poem, express your inner self; speak with a sweet tongue and be slow to anger; give a children's party; take ballroom dancing lessons..."'

© Ed Sullivan

After listening to a political speech on the TV nightly news and then watching the telecast's weather report, Fred Sevier of Sun City, Arizona, wondered how a meteorologist might report a political speech or some TV sermons. Possibly this way: "Beginning light and breezy with some intermittent hot air. Quickly becoming very windy, with gusts up to two hundred words a minute, and a jet stream of verbosity, with thoughts going counterclockwise around the central issue. Then becoming stormy, with much thunder but little enlightening; finally leading to a whirlwind conclusion, but leaving listeners in a fog."

⌀

Question: "What is the difference between a liturgist and a terrorist?"

Answer: "You can negotiate with a terrorist."

—Rev. Rawley Myers, Colorado Springs, Colorado

A preacher in our neck of the woods had just enjoyed a hearty chicken dinner at the home of one of his parishioners. Looking out the window after dinner, the preacher remarked, "That rooster of yours seems to be a mighty proud and happy bird." The host replied, "He should be. His oldest son just entered the ministry."

—Jim Reed, Cotter, Arkansas

A small boy, visiting the U.S. Senate with his father, asked him: "What does the chaplain do?"

"He stands up, looks at the Congress, and prays for the country," the father answered.

"I talked to a fellow not long ago who had been preaching in Kentucky. I asked where he'd been preaching. He said in Hazard, Kentucky. That's way back in the Appalachians, you know. He said it was so far back in the woods that even the Episcopalians were handling snakes."

—GEORGE GOLDTRAP

Question: Why did the Israelites wander forty years in the desert?
Answer: Even then men would not stop and ask for directions.

© Harley L. Schwadron

New churches:

Star Trek—The Next Denomination.

Church of the Independent Counsels.

—VIA PATTY WOOTEN, SANTA CRUZ, CALIFORNIA

A keynote speaker at a convention of priests came to the dais, shuffled his notes, scanned his audience, and said thoughtfully:

"Where to begin? Where to begin?"

A voice in the crowd yelled: "As close to the end as possible!"

—FR. NORMAN J. MUCKERMAN, CSSR, LIGUORI, MISSOURI

A well-liked minister in a small-town church was offered twice his salary to move to a large church in a big city.

A church member encountered the minister's daughter in a shop. "Is your father going to accept the church's offer in the big city?" the church member asked.

The daughter replied, "I don't know. He's been on his knees praying for divine guidance this morning."

"And what is your mother doing?"

"She's upstairs packing," the daughter said.

—VIA CATHERINE HALL, PITTSBURGH, PENNSYLVANIA

Philip Neri, a sixteenth-century Italian cleric known as "the clown-priest of Rome," always started his day with a prayer and this saying:

"A joke a day
And I'm on my way,
With no fear of tomorrow."

"There is nothing more miserable in the world than to arrive in Paradise and look like your passport photo."

—ERMA BOMBECK

At Christmastime a woman from Maine was visiting her family in a small town in the South. She was surprised to find in the town square a crèche with the three Wise Men wearing firefighters' helmets.

At a nearby church, she stopped and asked the secretary why the three Wise Men were wearing helmets. She said she couldn't recall reading anything about firefighters in the Bible's account of when Jesus was born.

"You Yankees never read the Bible!" the woman said, angrily. She took out a Bible, flipped through some pages, and pointed at a passage. "Look!" she said. "It says right here, 'The three Wise Men came from afar.'"

◎

After his air force and troops demolished Grozny, the capital of rebellious Chechnya, Russian President Boris Yeltsin was touring the area when he spotted an old Chechen man praying near the rubble of a home.

Yeltsin ordered his chauffeur to stop the limousine.

"You are praying for someone?" Yeltsin asked.

"I am praying for Boris Yeltsin," the old man replied.

"Thank you," Yeltsin said, identifying himself. "You seem old enough to have prayed for Stalin, Lenin, and the Czar. Did you pray for them, too?"

"Yes sir, I did," the old man replied. "And look what happened to them!"

⑥

My father grew up in a small Nebraska town, and one of his favorite stories was about Pastor Nelson. Each Sunday, during the announcements, Pastor Nelson asked everyone to fill out an attendance card and pass it to the side aisle.

The ushers collected the cards during the next hymn, which preceded the sermon. If the pastor forgot an important announcement, someone would write it on the back of a card and pass it to the ushers.

During the sermon, they would take the card to Pastor Nelson, who would read it to the congregation. One day they took him a note written by his wife. Without pause, Pastor Nelson announced to everyone, "Hurry up and get the sermon over with! The roast is burning!"

—BRUCE "CHARLIE" JOHNSON
EDITOR, *THE CLOWNIN' TIMES*, KENMORE, WASHINGTON

© Jonny Hawkins

Lois Blanchard Eades of Dickson, Tennessee, writes "Bib-limericks." Here are two of them:

> When Eve gave the apple to Adam,
> They did what Jehovah forbade 'em.
>> As might be expected,
>> When they were detected,
> He said, "Don't blame me; blame the madame."

> The animals entered with Noah;
> When God shut and bolted the doah,
>> The dinosaur cried,
>> "My wife is outside!"
> That's why dinosaurs are no moah.

@

"I can't find the books on Divine Guidance."

David A. Robb of Dalton, Georgia, passed on his thoughts on receiving Third Stanza, *an occasional paper of the Hymn Society in the United States and Canada:*

> I think that I shall never see
> a resurrected stanza three:
> The third, with oft the salient thought
> revealing why the hymn was wrought;
> The third, which sometimes bares the soul
> the hymnist wanted seen as whole;
> The third, replaced by interlude
> through which we stand in somber mood;
> "Let's sing the first, the second and last,
> the way we've done it in the past!"
> Hymns are sung by folk like me,
> but only God sings stanza three!

—DAVID A. ROBB, WITH APOLOGIES TO JOYCE KILMER

An old hellfire-and-brimstone preacher was always preaching that the worst was coming—maybe tomorrow. One day he asked a member of his church, "What would you say if I told you that tomorrow all the world's rivers and creeks were going to dry up?"

"Well," the man replied, "I'd say, 'Go thou and do likewise!'"

—George Goldtrap

SIGNS OF THE LAST DAYS

You know your days as pastor are numbered when…
- You're asked to be the donkey in the annual Christmas play.
- Without being asked, your secretary photocopies and sends your résumé to two hundred out-of-state churches.
- You find the visiting preacher's name on your mailbox.
- Shut-ins do not answer the doorbell when you visit.
- Your mother and your spouse move their membership letters to another church.
- Church members refer to you in the past tense.

- The pulpit committee that hired you starts wearing sackcloth.
- You come to church on Monday morning and find the locks have been changed.
- Your church splits, and the only thing the two groups can agree on is that neither group wants you as a pastor.

—VIA REV. KARL R. KRAFT, MANTUA, NEW JERSEY

"No pessimist ever discovered the secrets of the stars,
or sailed to an uncharted land,
or opened a new heaven to the human spirit.

—HELEN KELLER

Rev. John Burton, minister at Irving North Christian Church in Irving, Texas, shared these thoughts on the Y2K question in his church newsletter:

Am I going to sell my house, convert my entire estate into gold bullion, buy a truckload of freeze-dried foods and a few high-powered rifles, and move out to some deserted shack that I can light with a kerosene lantern (behind thick black curtains) and hide out until civilization falls and all the helpless and hapless people die?

On January 1, 2000, I will be right here in Irving, doing what God called me to do. If the world does come to an end, then I hope God will recognize that I did not desert my post at the hour of trial and tribulation.

Or if the city's computers all go down and there are shortages, then I want to be right here where I will be needed to help get things back to normal and see people through. Either way, I'll not run and hide. God will see me/us through.

If you are going to make provision for chaos coming from the Y2K thing, please remember your church:

Be Sure to Send in Your January and February Offerings, in Cash or Gold, Before December 31, 1999.

© Dik LaPine

"In a museum in Havana, there are two skulls of Christopher Columbus—one when he was a boy and one when he was a man."

—MARK TWAIN

A pastor was talking to the church organist. "When I finish my sermon," he said, "I'll ask for all those in the congregation who want to contribute four hundred dollars toward the church's mortgage to stand up. In the meantime, you can provide appropriate music."

"Any suggestions?" the organist asked.

"You might try 'The Star-Spangled Banner,'" the pastor replied.

⑥

Rev. Warren Keating, pastor of First Presbyterian Church, Derby, Kansas, told this story:

There once was a very rich man who "wanted to take it with him" when he died. He prayed and prayed until finally the Lord gave in, but on one condition—he could only bring one suitcase of his wealth.

The rich man then began to worry: "What kind of currency should I bring—the dollar, the pound, the yen, the mark?" He finally decided that the best thing to do was to turn all his wealth into gold bullion.

The day came when God called him home. St. Peter greeted him, but told him he couldn't bring his suitcase in with him.

"I have an agreement with God that I can take it with me," the man explained.

"That's unusual," St. Peter said. "This has never happened before. Mind if I take a look?"

The man opened the suitcase to reveal the shining gold bullion.

"*Pavement!*" the amazed St. Peter exclaimed. "Why in the world would you bring *pavement?*"

⑥

Bumper sticker spotted by George Goldtrap, Ormond-by-the-Sea, Florida:

"*The More You Complain, the Longer God Lets You Live.*"

⑥

"About all I can say about the United States Senate is that it opens with a prayer and closes with an investigation."

—WILL ROGERS

This is "The Clown's Prayer" of Smiles Unlimited, a clown ministry to hospitals, nursing homes, and prisons, based in Indianapolis:

"Lord, as I stumble through this life, help me to create more laughter than tears, dispense more happiness than gloom, spread more cheer than despair. Never let me become so indifferent that I fail to see the wonder in the eyes of a child or the twinkle in the eyes of the aged. Never let me forget that my total effort is to cheer people, make them happy, and help them forget at least for a moment all the unpleasant things in their lives. And, Lord, in my final moment, may I hear you whisper: 'When you made My people smile, you made Me smile.'"

—DON ("SKI") AND RUBY ("TAH-DAH!") BERKOSKI

Sign outside a church in the Midwest:
>*"Do You Know What Hell Is Like?*
>*Come In and Hear Our Choir."*

Over the great front doors of an old church being restored was inscribed in stone: "This Is the Gate of Heaven." Just below it, someone had placed a small cardboard sign that read: "Use Other Entrance."

Seen on a church sign:
>*"If Evolution Is True,*
>*Why Do Mothers Still Have Only Two Hands?"*

—REV. TIM DAVIS
WESTMOUNT PARK CHURCH, TORONTO, CANADA

Bob Heltman of Hendersonville, North Carolina, spotted this bumper sticker on a car:

"If God Can Make It on 10%, Why Not the Government?"

🌀

Sign seen on the front lawn of a church in Brentwood, California:

"For Sale By Owner."

🌀

Marius Risley of Buffalo, New York, saw this sign in an Episcopal church parking lot:

"Clergy Space
You Park
You Preach."

Sister Mary Christelle Macaluso, RSM, also known as "The Fun Nun," who lives in Omaha, Nebraska, says she once drove by a church sign that read:

"Jesus Saves."

Directly across the street was a grocery store sign:

"We Save You More!"

A gospel group called "The Resurrection" was scheduled to sing at the Barlow (Kentucky) First Baptist Church, but the performance was postponed because of a snowstorm. The pastor put up a sign outside that read: "The Resurrection Is Postponed."

—VIA MARIA VILLALOVOS, PICO RIVERA, CALIFORNIA

On a sign in front of Emmanuel Baptist Church in Waco, Texas:

> *"Welcome to Eternity—Smoking or Non-Smoking?"*
>
> —GEORGE GOLDTRAP

Hazel Bimler of Itasca, Illinois, spotted this sign at Christmastime at Women's Workout World:

> *"Merry Fitness—Happy New Rear!"*

Sign in a Marshall, Michigan, ice cream parlor:
> *"Notice:*
> *If You Are Grouchy, Irritable,*
> *or Just Plain Mean,*
> *There Will Be a $10.00 Charge*
> *for Putting Up with You."*
>
> —VIA MATT SAMRA

© Jonny Hawkins

In Sioux Falls, South Dakota, they call FMC member Rev. Jeff Hayes "Pastor Pun." Hayes amuses and cheers up passersby with the daily puns and witticisms he puts up on the outdoor sign of Faith Temple Church.

Hayes now has a collection of over five hundred sayings for church signs. Here are some of them:

- "Church Ushers Always Pass the Buck."
- "Wanted: Large Mouth Bass for Church Choir."
- "Come On In and Tithe One On During the Offering."
- "Old Deacons Never Die; They Continue to Make Motions."
- "Trashed? God Can Recycle You."
- "Confessions from Weekend Fishermen Heard Every Monday."
- "The Pits of Life Can Sprout a Peach of a Person."

- "Soul Food Served at Every Service."
- "We Welcome All Denominations—$1, $5, $10, $20, $50, $100."
- "Happy Hour Now in Progress."
- "The King of Hearts Enables One to Play with a Full Deck."
- "Shepherds of the Flock Never Fleece their Sheep."
- "The Heart of God Is Never in Need of a Bypass."
- "The Great Physician Still Makes House Calls."
- "If You Think You're Too Cool for God, You'll Warm Up."
- "On Pins and Needles? Jesus Will Cushion You."
- "Getting Old? Jesus Can Put a New Wrinkle in Your Life."
- "Sorry but the Fruit of the Spirit Doesn't Include Sour Grapes."

- "Spiritual Health and Fitness Club."
- "Christmas: It's a Boy!"
- "Easter: No Gloom in the Tomb."
- "Hope Causes the Son to Rise in Our Mourning."

A worldly unbeliever engaged the first Trappist abbot of Gethsemane in conversation. "I never go to church, Abbot," the man said. "There are too many hypocrites there."

"Oh, don't let that keep you away," smiled the abbot. "There's always room for one more, you know."

—REV. BRUNO M. HAGSPIEL, SVD

> *"We are all here for a spell.*
> *Get all the good laughs you can."*
>
> —WILL ROGERS

About ten o'clock one cold February morning, a man was in bed sound asleep. His mother came into the room.

"Son, it's time to get up. You gotta get ready for church," she implored.

"I'm too tired. Leave me alone," he said.

"Son, you gotta get up and get ready for church."

"I'm not going to church. Give me one good reason why I have to go to church," he protested.

"I'll give you two good reasons: one, it's Sunday, and two, you're the pastor!"

—VIA DEACON WILLIAM MCAVOY, LENEXA, KANSAS

6

"I think it's important that we Catholics preserve our identity. Penance is important. With the shortage of priests, maybe we should have a drive-through at our churches to speed up confession.

"You pull up in the family van. You have the whole family with you. The priest says over the microphone: 'In the name of the Father and the Son and the Holy Spirit.'

"You say into the microphone: 'Bless me, Father, for I have sinned. I had a Number 5. The wife had a Number 9. My daughter had a Number 8. And my son had a combo—5, 8, and 9.'"

—TOMMY DINARDO, CATHOLIC COMEDIAN, VIRGINIA
     BEACH, VIRGINIA

Toward the end of his life, when he was suffering from the accumulated effects of a lifetime of drinking, an ill W. C. Fields was discovered reading the Bible by one of his friends.

The astonished friend asked: "What are you—an atheist—doing reading the Bible?"

"I'm looking for loopholes," Fields replied.

A missionary heard about a native who had five wives. "You are violating a law of God," he said, "so you must go and tell four of those women they can no longer live here or consider you their husband."

The native thought a few moments. Then he said, "I'll wait here. You tell 'em."

—TAL BONHAM

A pastor, disappointed that things were not "happening" in his church, asked a deacon, "What's wrong with our church? Is it ignorance or apathy?"

The deacon replied, "I don't know and I don't care!"

—REV. STUART A. SCHLEGEL, SANTA CRUZ, CALIFORNIA

Without informing his wife, an Anglican priest invited his bishop to stay overnight at his home after a confirmation. Before supper, the bishop was walking down a dimly lit corridor in the priest's home. The priest's wife, coming up from behind, mistook the bishop for her husband and gave him a clout over the ear. "That'll teach you to ask the bishop to stay when we've got nothing in the house," she snapped.

—THE ANGLICAN DIGEST

"We were called to be witnesses, not lawyers."

—DONA MADDUX COOPER, STILLWATER, OKLAHOMA

Received in the morning mail:

And Jesus said, "Who do you say I am?"

And they answered: "You are the eschatological manifestation of the ground of our being, the *kerygma* in which we found the ultimate meaning of our interpersonal relationship."

And Jesus said, "What?"

"The duty of a toastmaster is to be so dull that the succeeding speakers will appear brilliant by contrast."

—CLARENCE B. KELLAND

POLITICALLY CORRECT LORD'S PRAYER

"Our Universal Chairperson in outer space, Your identity enjoys the highest rating on a prioritized selectivity scale. May Your sphere of influence take on reality parameters; may Your mindset be implemented on this planet as in outer space.

"Allot to us at this point in time and on a per diem basis, a sufficient and balanced dietary food intake, and rationalize a disclaimer against our negative feedback as we rationalize the negative feedback of others.

"And deprogram our negative potentialities, but desensitize the impact of the counterproductive force. For Yours is the dominant sphere of influence, the ultimate capability, and the highest qualitative analysis rating, at this point in time and extending beyond a limited time frame. End of message."

"My wife has been bugging me about church. But, hey, I've got my whole life ahead of me. There's plenty of time for religion."

© Ed Sullivan

A preacher's car broke down on a country road, far away from everything but a small tavern. When he walked inside to use the phone, he saw his old friend Hank, shabbily dressed and drunk, sitting at the bar.

"Hank, what happened?" the preacher asked. "You used to be a prosperous man."

Hank told him about all the problems he had experienced and the bad investments he had made and asked the pastor's advice.

"Go home," the preacher said. "And when you get there, open your Bible and put your finger down on the page. God will give you the answer."

A year later, the preacher saw Hank wearing an expensive new suit and getting into a new Mercedes. "I'm glad to see that things turned around for you," the preacher said.

"They sure have, and I owe it all to you, Pastor," Hank said. "I went home, like you said, opened my Bible, put my finger down on the page, and there was the answer: Chapter 11."

—REV. WARREN J. KEATING
FIRST PRESBYTERIAN CHURCH, DERBY, KANSAS

"It's been suggested that the IRS post signs in its offices that read: 'In God we trust. Everyone else is subject to an audit.'"

—CHARLES J. MILAZZO, ST. PETERSBURG, FLORIDA

In the beginning, God created heaven and earth. He was challenged immediately with a class-action suit for failure to file an environmental impact statement.

At last, He was granted a temporary permit for the project, but soon was handed a cease-and-desist order enjoining Him from creating on earth.

At the government hearing, God said, "Let there be light." The bureaucrats demanded to know how the light would be made. They asked if there would be thermal pollution or strip mining.

God replied that the light would be created from a huge ball of fire. God was granted provisional permission to make light (1) if He would obtain a building permit, (2) if no smoke would result from the ball of fire, and (3) if He would keep the light on only half the time to conserve energy.

God agreed and said He would call the light "day" and the darkness "night."

Then God said, "Let the earth bring forth green herbs and many seeds." The EPA agreed, as long as native seed was used.

Then God said, "Let waters bring forth creeping creatures having life; and the fowl that may fly over the earth." Officials insisted that this would require approval from the Department of Fish and Game.

When God said He wanted to complete the project in six days, the officials informed Him it would take at least two hundred days to review the application and the environmental impact statement. Then there would be a public hearing followed by a twelve-month waiting period.

Then God created hell.

—VIA FMC MEMBER STEVE FELDMAN, JEFFERSON CITY, MISSOURI, ORIGINAL AUTHOR UNKNOWN

A PASTOR'S PRAYER

Lord, fill my mouth
With worthwhile stuff
And nudge me
When I've said enough.

—VIA REV. JACK E. MUSICK, NARROWS, VIRGINIA

The minister, leading prayers, was being carried away by his own exuberance. He began: "O Thou, who rulest the raging of the sea and calmest the fierceness of the winds…" He then seemed to lose himself for a moment, but soon carried on: "…bless our wives."

—THE *DESERT WIND*, SCOTTSDALE, ARIZONA

© Ed Sullivan

The ship was sinking fast. The captain called out, "Anyone here know how to pray?"

One man stepped forward: "I do, Captain."

"Good," said the captain. "You pray. The rest of us will put on life preservers. We're one short."

—Archbishop John L. May of St. Louis, Missouri

When FMC member Rev. Robert M. Ross, rector of Saint Peter's Episcopal Church, Osterville, Massachusetts, arrived at seminary, he noticed that someone had put up on the bulletin board a small sign with the simple message: "Job 7:11."

Supposing that it was a scriptural word of encouragement for seminarians, similar to John 3:16, Ross noted the citation and went home to look it up. It read: "Therefore I will not restrain my mouth; I will speak in the anguish of my spirit; I will complain in the bitterness of my soul" (NRSV).

"How terribly this person must be suffering!" Ross thought, wondering if the sign was a cry for help. The next day he took his concerns to the chaplain.

"Oh, that was on the employment board," the chaplain smiled. "There's a job opening at the Seven-Eleven."

"After God created the world, He made man and woman. Then, to keep the whole thing from collapsing, He invented humor."
—Mordillo

—VIA BILL KELLY, DEERFIELD, ILLINOIS

There was this nice lady mailing the old family Bible to her brother in another part of the country.

"Is there anything breakable in here?" asked the postal clerk.

"Only the Ten Commandments," said the lady.

The obituary editor of a Boston newspaper was not one who would easily admit his mistakes. One day, he got a phone call from an irate subscriber who complained that his name just appeared in the obituary column. "Really?" was the calm reply. "Where are you calling from?"

—ARCHBISHOP JOHN L. MAY

The gate between heaven and hell broke down. St. Peter appeared at the broken part and called out to the devil, "Hey, Satan. It's your turn to fix it this time."

"Sorry," replied the devil, "my people are too busy to go about fixing a mere gate."

"Well, then," said St. Peter, "I'll have to sue you for breaking our agreement."

"Oh yeah?" said the devil. "Where are you going to get a lawyer?"

—MSGR. ARTHUR TONNE, *JOKES PRIESTS CAN TELL*

A man and a woman, who were friends for many years, died and went to heaven. They told St. Peter they wanted to get married.

"Take your time and think about it," St. Peter said. "You have an eternity to think about it here. Come back and talk to me about it in fifty years."

Fifty years later, the couple returned and again told St. Peter they wanted to get married.

"Take your time and think some more about it," St. Peter said. "Come back and see me in another fifty years, and if we don't have a preacher up here by then, I'll marry you myself."

—REV. PAUL R. COLEMAN, ZELIENOPLE, PENNSYLVANIA

FMC member Rev. Donald R. Jafvert, pastor of the Chapel by the Sea, Ft. Myers Beach, Florida, once attended a continuing education event at Trinity College in Dublin, Ireland, location of the famous library which is home to the *Book of Kells* and other very old church manuscripts.

While visiting the men's restroom, he noted this message written on the inside of a stall door:

"This is a new door. The previous door, due to its literary capacity having been reached, was designated ISBN 0-37-078945-A and taken away for binding. It will shortly be published in paperback."

IF YOU WISH TO SPEAK WITH GOD, PLEASE PRESS 1

Fr. Dominic Maruca, SJ, a professor at Pontifical Gregorian University in Rome, wrote in *The Priest* magazine that one day he was having difficulty with a new computer and called the 800 number provided by the manufacturer.

While waiting for a human voice to come on the line, Fr. Maruca began to daydream: "What would it be like if terrestrial hi-tech finally reached the heavenly realms, for example, when I tried to pray?"

In his daydream, Fr. Maruca said he heard this recording:

"Thank you for calling technical support. We are available to assist you every day of the week except, of course, on the Sabbath. If you have a Touch Tone telephone, you can reach your desired party by pressing the appropriate number.

"If you wish to speak with God the Father, please press 1.

"If you wish to speak with Jesus, His Son, please press 2.

"If you wish to speak with His Holy Spirit, please press 3.

"If you wish to speak with Mary, the mother of Jesus, please press 4.

"If you wish to speak with one of the saints, please press 5.

"If you have some question about the Ten Commandments, press 6.

"If you have some complaint about the liturgical changes, please press 7.

> "If your trouble is with the Church Universal,
> press 8.
>
> "If you are having difficulty with your local
> bishop or pastor, press 9."

Fr. Maruca said he awakened from his daydream somewhat shaken. After shutting down his printer and computer, he went down to the chapel. As he knelt there, he thought he heard a chuckle coming from the direction of the tabernacle. It was probably just his overactive imagination.

Anyway, he caught himself smiling and heard himself saying, "Thanks, Lord, for always being so readily accessible. Please don't go hi-tech on us—ever."

"Make a joyful noise to the LORD, all the lands."

—PSALM 100:1 (RSV)

The U. S. Postal Service affixed this yellow adhesive label on an envelope returned to a mailer because it could not be delivered:

> *KING380   92028028 3989   10/21/89*
> *RETURN TO SENDER*
> *CHRIST THE KING*
> *MOVED LEFT NO ADDRESS*
> *UNABLE TO FORWARD*
> *RETURN TO SENDER POST DUE = $.25*

"If you're going to be able to look back on something and laugh about it, you might as well laugh at it now."

—MARIE OSMOND

If you enjoyed this gift book, ask for the others at your local bookstore…

From the Mouths of Babes, ISBN: 1-57856-284-8

Rolling in the Aisles, ISBN: 1-57856-285-6

The Laughter Prescription, ISBN: 1-57856-286-4

…as well as the full-length paperbacks from which they were drawn:

Holy Humor, ISBN: 1-57856-279-1

More Holy Humor, ISBN: 1-57856-280-5

Holy Hilarity, ISBN: 1-57856-281-3

More Holy Hilarity, ISBN: 1-57856-282-1

WATERBROOK
PRESS